Corruption and the Church
A Brief Introduction

The M-series is a collection of short, accessible papers and articles from Micah Global, being developed in response to the need for clear, authoritative statements on key themes. They form a foundation of historical and current ideas that contribute to our understanding and practice of integral mission. They aim to promote reflection, dialogue, articulation and action on the major concepts and issues that move us towards transforming mission.

The M-series is an essential resource for practitioners, theologians, students, leaders, and teachers.

M-Series from im:press

Titles in print:
Integral Mission: Biblical Foundations
by Melba Maggay

The Five Marks of Mission:
Making God's Mission Ours
by Chris Wright

Towards Transformed Honour
by Arley Loewen

Living in God's Story:
Understanding the Bible's Grand Narrative
by Mark Galpin

Corruption and the Church
A Brief Introduction

Martin Allaby

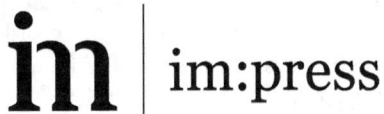

Copyright © Martin Allaby
The author asserts the moral right to be identified as the author of this work

Published by im:press An imprint of Micah Global

ISBN: 978-1-4855-0008-7

All rights reserved.
No part of this book may be transmitted or reproduced in any form or by any means, including but not restricted to photocopying, recording, or by any information storage and retrieval system, without written permission from the publisher; except for brief quotations in printed reviews.

Printed and bound by Ingram Spark

What is corruption?

THERE is no universally agreed definition of corruption, but many people use this definition from Transparency International: 'the abuse of entrusted power for private gain'. This definition includes both legal and illegal behaviour; the public and private sectors; and visible forms of corruption, such as bribery, as well as less visible forms, such as cronyism. But to keep its focus, this definition stops short of including all injustice, all inequality and all failures in ethics or integrity. Transparency International classifies corruption as grand, petty or political, depending on the amounts of money lost, and the sector where it occurs:

> *Grand corruption* consists of acts committed at a high level of government that distort policies or the central functioning of the state, enabling leaders to benefit at the expense of the public good.
>
> *Petty corruption* refers to everyday abuse of entrusted power by low- and mid-level public officials in their interactions with ordinary citizens, who often are trying to access basic goods or services in places like hospitals, schools, police departments and other agencies.
>
> *Political corruption* is a manipulation of policies, institutions and rules of procedure in the allocation of resources and financing by political decision makers, who abuse their position to sustain their power, status and wealth.

Petty corruption often has its roots in poverty, because the salaries of those who are corrupt are too low to meet their basic needs. Although it is usually illegal, those involved may not see it as wrong if their culture has a long-established tradition of giving gifts when doing business. Careful assessment of the power balance between the parties involved, and their gains and losses from the transaction, can help to clarify the ethics involved. For example, a parent who is forced by a hospital worker to give an illegal payment to get essential treatment for their sick child should be seen as a victim of extortion, not a corrupt person.

Grand corruption and political corruption, on the other hand, are rooted in greed for power or money. They may be perfectly legal, simply because those who are corrupt have enough influence to ensure that the law does not define their corrupt acts as illegal. For example, the UK has been very slow to change its laws to make it more difficult for corrupt money to be hidden in banks within its territories. The UK also has few restrictions on the revolving door between government and business, which allows elites to design government policies that favour the interests of a specific business, then take up a well-paid job in that business. One UK critic has observed that:

> For organisations such as the World Bank and the World Economic Forum, there is little difference between the public interest and the interests of global corporations. What might look like corruption from any other perspective looks to them like sound economics. The power of global finance and the immense wealth of the global elite are founded on corruption, and the beneficiaries have an interest in framing the question to excuse themselves.

> Yes, many poor nations are plagued by the kind of corruption that involves paying bribes to officials. But the problems plaguing us run deeper. When the system already belongs to the elite, bribes are superfluous.

Although corruption exists in all countries, when organisations such as Transparency International give them scores for control of corruption, some countries receive much better scores than others. These scores are quite good at predicting whether governments use the money they control to benefit ordinary citizens rather than just a few elites; they clearly tell us something useful about how ruling elites behave towards their own citizens.

> Many poor nations are plagued by the kind of corruption that involves paying bribes to officials. But the problems plaguing us in the UK run deeper. When the system already belongs to the elite, bribes are superfluous.

However, many people want their governments to serve the interests of people worldwide, not just their own citizens, and corruption scores are less likely to capture that concern. Joseph Stiglitz, for example, the Nobel economist who chaired US President Clinton's Council of Economic Advisers, explained that the United States used very different criteria when considering whether domestic pension funds should be contracted out to the private sector, depending on whether the pensions funds belonged to US citizens, or citizens of other countries.

When choosing the best policy for the pension funds of US citizens, the criteria for decision making were fairness and efficiency, and they decided that the best way of meeting these criteria would be by keeping the pension funds in the public sector. However, when they came to choosing the best policy for the pension funds of people from other countries, the sole criterion for decision making was 'What is good for America?'

Using that criterion, they advised that foreign pension funds should be contracted out to the private sector, because this would create business opportunities and employment for US citizens. This sort of policy-making process does not affect the US score for control of corruption (because the exercise of public power served the public interest in the US); but the process does not serve the public interest in other countries, and citizens of those countries might see it as corrupt.

What does the Bible say about corruption?

I have found that Christians from high-income countries focus more on the 'unrighteousness' of ordinary people in poorer countries who are forced to pay bribes for essential services, and much less on trying to change the unjust systems that allow such extortion to happen. We need to ask whether this reflects the balance of biblical material about corruption.

One Christian spent a year reading through the Bible twice, noting the passages that are relevant to corruption. These passages appear in a wide range of the books in the Bible. They are found most frequently in Proverbs and the Prophets, followed by the New Testament, the five books of the Law and the Psalms. He concluded that the Bible passages that talk about corruption fall into five main categories:

> **The Bible's condemnation of corruption is directed particularly towards the rich and powerful.**

- Bribery. For example, Micah 7:3 – 'Officials and judges alike demand bribes. The people with influence get what they want, and together they scheme to twist justice.'

- Denial of justice, particularly in relation to rulings in court. For example, Isaiah 10:1-3 – 'What sorrow awaits the unjust judges and those who issue unfair laws. They deprive the poor of justice and deny the rights of the needy among my people. They prey on widows and take advantage of orphans.'

- Oppression, including arbitrary behaviour outside the law. For example, Ezekiel 45:9 – 'For this is what the Sovereign Lord says: Enough, you princes of Israel! Stop your violence and oppression and do what is just and right. Quit robbing and cheating my people out of their land. Stop expelling them from their homes, says the Sovereign Lord'.

- Gaining wealth by unjust means. For example, 1 Cor 6:9-10 – 'Don't you realise that those who do wrong will not inherit the Kingdom of God? Don't fool yourselves. Those who ... are thieves, or greedy people, ..., or who cheat people – none of these will inherit the Kingdom of God'.

- Dishonesty. For example, Zech 8:16-17 – 'But this is what you must do: Tell the truth to each other. Render verdicts in your courts that are just and that lead to peace. Don't scheme against each other. Stop your love of telling lies that you swear are the truth. I hate all these things, says the Lord'.

Most of the five categories above deal with opportunities that are available mainly to elites: judges, who can deny justice in court; rulers, who have the power to oppress others; and people who have become rich by unjust means. And with bribery, the Bible's condemnation is targeted at elites who use their wealth to offer bribes, or their official position to demand them, rather than the poor who are forced to pay bribes by corrupt officials. Indeed, the latter kind of 'bribery' is usually a response to extortion, rather than initiation of a corrupt transaction.

An important biblical word in this context is the Hebrew *sedeq*, which was usually translated in the Greek New Testament as *dikaiosynē*. Both words refer to *good behaviour within a community*, rather than the abstract idea of justice or virtue. The English language lacks a single word that captures this biblical concept, so in English Bibles it is usually translated as either 'justice' or 'righteousness', and the choice of English word says as much about the translator as about the text itself.

Matthew 5:10, for example, comes across differently when translated as 'Blessed are those who are persecuted for the sake of justice,' as opposed to the much more common translation, 'Blessed are those who are persecuted for the sake of righteousness.' As one theologian has observed: 'How many people do you know that have been persecuted for morally upright living? I have never seen that. The people who are persecuted are the ones that seek justice.'

> The harmful effects of corruption are especially severe on the poor, who are hardest hit by economic decline and are most reliant on the provision of public services.

Why is it important to control corruption?

THIS statement from the World Bank describes the damaging effects of corruption on whole economies, and especially on the poor:

> It is among the greatest obstacles to economic and social development. It undermines development by distorting the rule of law and weakening the institutional foundation on which economic growth depends. The harmful effects of corruption are especially severe on the poor, who are hardest hit by economic decline, are most reliant on the provision of public services, and are least capable of paying the extra costs associated with bribery, fraud, and the misappropriation of economic privileges. Corruption sabotages policies and programs that aim to reduce poverty.

When David Cameron was Prime Minister of the UK in 2015 he said this about corruption:

> Corruption is the cancer at the heart of so many of the problems we face around the world today. The migrants drowning in the Mediterranean are fleeing from corrupt African states. Efforts to address global poverty are too often undermined by corrupt governments preventing people getting the revenues and benefits of growth that are rightfully theirs. The World Economic Forum estimates that corruption adds 10% to business costs globally, while the World Bank believes some $1 trillion is paid in bribes every year.

Corruption doesn't just threaten our prosperity, it also undermines our security. Whether it is the abduction of schoolgirls in Nigeria or the recruitment of fighters to the Taliban and Islamic State, time and again ordinary people are drawn to extremist groups partly as a reaction to the oppression and corruption of their own governments. World leaders simply cannot dodge this issue any longer.

Another reason why Christians in particular should try to control corruption is that it can protect people from having to choose between paying a bribe (which may leave them with a bad conscience), or losing access to essentials such as healthcare for their children.

Why do some countries have less corruption than others?

THE first thing to note is that national corruption scores such as those produced by Transparency International are strongly correlated with national income: rich countries have better scores for control of corruption. That raises the question, did rich countries become rich because they were better at controlling corruption? Or were there other factors, such as their geography, the wild plants and animals available for farming, or exploitation of other countries through slavery and other means, that allowed them to become rich first, with improvements in control of corruption coming only later?

Academics have debated this at length and it seems that all these factors have played important roles in economic development. For example, it seems that white colonialists in Africa adopted different strategies according to their risk of death from malaria and other tropical diseases. In countries such as the Congo, where death rates were high, European colonialists had little interest in living there and just used whatever brutal means they wanted to make money, such as 'incentivising' rubber growers by cutting off their hands if they failed to deliver their quotas of rubber on time.

Conversely, in countries such as South Africa or Zambia, colonialists faced much lower risks of death and were happy to settle in the country. It was in their economic interest to establish laws and institutions that would help them keep legal control of the land and assets they acquired, and those laws and institutions continue to support economic development and help control corruption today.

After national income, the two factors that best explain national corruption scores are colonial rule and democracy. After adjusting for per capita GDP, a history of colonial rule by the UK is associated with substantially lower levels of corruption. One academic has observed that the British are inclined to treat rules and procedures like sacred rituals so that judges, for example, will follow procedures even when the results threaten those in power, which increases the chance that official corruption will be exposed. Perhaps surprisingly, there is no clear evidence of lower levels of corruption in countries that have never been colonised, such as Thailand or Nepal. This suggests that grand corruption is carried out by ruling elites of all kinds, whether indigenous or colonial.

Another surprise is that democracy needs to be in place without interruption for several decades before it starts to show any benefits in terms of better control of corruption. The relative lack of effect of democracy may reflect the reality that politicians need to strike informal deals with their backers while they are fund-raising to compete in elections, and those backers will seek political favours in return if their candidate wins.

Protestant Christians will be happy to know that countries with a larger proportion of Protestants have slightly lower levels of corruption. One explanation for this is that Protestants emphasise personal responsibility for avoiding sin, while the Catholic church places more emphasis on the inherent weakness of human beings, their inability to escape sin, and the need for the church to be forgiving and protecting. An alternative explanation is that Protestantism arose through protest against centralised religious authority, and societies with a culture of protest in religious matters are more inclined to challenge abuse of authority in the political sphere.

It is important to remember that all the correlations described here are statistical, not deterministic. So, although there are some countries that are exceptions to the general rule, those exceptions do not invalidate the rule. They simply suggest that some other local factors were at work in those countries.

How does this relate to integral mission?

MICAH Global describes integral mission as:

> the proclamation and demonstration of the gospel. It is not simply that evangelism and social involvement are to be done alongside each other. Rather, in integral mission our proclamation has social consequences as we call people to love and repentance in all areas of life. And our social involvement has evangelistic consequences as we bear witness to the transforming grace of Jesus Christ.

Given the definition of corruption as 'the abuse of entrusted power for private gain', it is clear that those who respond to this call to love and repentance by trying to fight corruption will quickly come up against ungodly powers that oppose them. Although almost everyone is better off when corruption is controlled, apart from a few elites who lose out financially, efforts to fight corruption are hindered by a 'prime mover' problem: any leader who starts to fight against corruption is likely to be persecuted for their efforts, and that deters many people. This will obviously be true for a community leader with integrity who decides to love their community by protesting against corruption.

Slightly less obviously, it will also be true for a corrupt member of the elite who repents. It is relatively

> Any leader who starts to fight against corruption is likely to be persecuted for their efforts. Jesus Christ, more than anyone else in history, has shown us what it means to accept suffering so that others may benefit.

rare to find corrupt individuals who act alone in systems that function legitimately and serve the public interest. Much more commonly, they are just one cog in a complex system of corruption; even the president of one African nation was described by a well-informed observer as 'a dog on a leash'. If such a person repents, they will certainly pay a price as those remaining in the corrupt system around them seek to preserve and protect their interests.

Jesus Christ, more than anyone else in history, has shown us what it means to accept suffering so that others may benefit. Through his resurrection, God has demonstrated that his sacrifice was worthwhile and that the forces of evil do not have the last word. As Bishop Tutu reminded people while holding up his Bible during the years of apartheid in South Africa, 'I have read this book to the end, and we win!'

Why aren't Christians more involved in fighting corruption?

A few years ago, a Christian colleague published this critique of the lack of engagement by religious, including Christian, organisations in the fight against corruption:

> Surprisingly, corruption is receiving far more attention from 'secular' organisations than religious ones. While faith leaders and organisations are increasingly engaged across much of the development agenda, particularly in the areas of HIV/AIDS and education, they are generally less active in the governance and anti-corruption arena. Given corruption's profound moral and social justice dimensions, religious groups should be at the forefront of this struggle.

It is certainly true that most Christians are more inclined to engage in their own aid or relief activities than to get involved in fighting corruption. Relief efforts are essential following natural disasters, and aid may be the only option open to Christians in countries where they are persecuted for their faith, or where dictatorial rulers oppress all their citizens. However, there are many countries where Christians have sufficient freedom to fight corruption, but instead they continue to focus on aid. Why is this?

For nearly twenty years I have been listening, either informally or as part of a formal research project, to what people say about why Christians are not particularly engaged in fighting corruption. Although dualistic theology (the idea that God is only interested in saving souls to send to heaven) is often part of the problem, there are a number of much more down-to-earth explanations:

You might be accused of hypocrisy

Many Christians I have interviewed admit to problems of corruption within churches. It has been estimated that US$ 50 billion per annum may be stolen from money that Christians give to churches, para-church organisations, and secular organisations around the world. I vividly remember having lunch with an African Evangelical leader in 2006, as I was about to design some country case studies looking at ways in which Protestants might be helping to reduce corruption. He warned me that I might be disappointed if I came to Africa, telling me that in his country the churches were high on the government's list of institutions that should be investigated for corruption.

Your church might lose money

Another Christian told me that a pastor in his community who knows that a wealthy member of their congregation obtained their wealth through corrupt means will be reluctant to preach against it, because they know that wealthy member can move to another church that won't make them feel uncomfortable.

> It has been estimated that US$ 50 billion per annum may be stolen from money that Christians give to churches, para-church organisations, and secular organisations around the world.

You might be killed

Among the 101 people I have interviewed formally about fighting corruption, three were survivors of assassination attempts. Jovita Salonga, former President of the Philippine Senate, was critically injured in a bomb attack after conducting enquiries into government corruption. David Gitari, former Anglican Archbishop of Kenya, survived an attempted lynching after campaigning against electoral abuses. A Zambian church leader described a drive-by shooting after he refused to support the President's campaign for re-election.

You might lose your job

A South Korean Christian who worked as a tax official described what happened after he decided to stop asking for bribes. He no longer had any bribe money to pass up the line to his boss, so he was punished by being transferred to a remote region, with no schooling for his children.

It takes too long to change anything

Although there are exceptions, such as Singapore, commentators observe that real improvements in the control of corruption typically take one or two generations. This is not an activity for those who expect quick results.

It is difficult to evaluate impact

Even when measures of corruption improve, as happened with Transparency International's CPI score for the Philippines in the context of substantial anti-corruption efforts by Christians, it can be challenging to prove cause and effect.

It is much easier to ignore corruption and start an aid project instead

Not only can you avoid all the problems above, but the beneficiaries of your project will be grateful, and if you get donor funding you can create jobs for local Christians. However, there are two big problems with this approach. First, in most countries the resources that the government raises locally from taxes and charges vastly exceed the total amount of aid the country receives from all sources. So if Christians

> 'When Christians allow themselves to be pre-occupied by 'aid', rather than focussing on fighting corruption where that is a realistic option, they may actually be perpetuating poverty.'

really want to help the poor, then focussing on aid, rather than on what the government does with its own resources, is missing the main issue.

The second big problem is that corruption hinders economic growth and perpetuates poverty. In short, when Christians allow themselves to be pre-occupied by 'aid', rather than focussing on fighting corruption where that is a realistic option, they may actually be perpetuating poverty.

Some Christians may ask 'But didn't Jesus say "The poor will always be with you"?' Yes, in the context of rebuking Judas for his scornful attitude toward a woman for pouring out her expensive perfume on Jesus before his crucifixion. But he was quoting Deuteronomy 15:11, which follows just a few verses after Deuteronomy 15:4-5: 'There need be no poor people among you, for in the land the Lord your God is giving you to possess as your inheritance, he will richly bless you, if only you fully obey the Lord your God and are careful to follow all these commands I am giving you today'. Those commands, of course, include all the Bible's prohibitions against corruption. As Christians we should not use Jesus' words as an excuse to ignore poverty or corruption.

What can Christians do to fight corruption?

Start within the body of Christ

A useful starting point here is the list of recommendations on pages 166-191 of Christoph Stückelberger's book 'Corruption-free Churches are Possible' (available free online – please see 'recommended further reading' at the end of this book). Stückelberger organises his recommendations under the following headings:

- Theology, Ecclesiology and Ethics
- Leadership and Governance
- Stewardship of Resources and Projects
- Preaching, Teaching and Educating
- Gender Equity and Women's Empowerment
- Sanctions and Courts
- Media, Campaigns, Databases, Networks and Programmes.

Case study: Operation Nehemiah (India)

Since 2012 the Operation Nehemiah movement in India has been operating as a holistic movement for financial accountability and integrity for the church in India. It serves primarily through leadership and culture interventions, and facilitating organisational processes of introspection and change, starting with the top leadership.

Their ethos is one of *feet washing* rather than *finger pointing*. As they seek to assist the church in finding answers to questions about financial integrity, they emphasise that Christian leadership and integrity (including financial) is first of all a matter of the heart. They believe that there are clear biblical principles about handling money and finances, but they also teach that each organisation must seek God and his Word and tread its own journey to find solutions specific to them.

They have run national and regional events for church leaders to review the Biblical Foundations for financial integrity, and to sensitise and motivate church leaders about the issue. They also offer customised interventions for leaders of large denominations to help initiate change; facilitate peer groups that can counter leader loneliness and vulnerability; and foster sharing of best practices and help for specific issues.

> Operation Nehemiah is a holistic movement for financial accountability and integrity for the Church in India. Their ethos is one of foot washing rather than finger pointing.

The deep-seated changes that the Operation Nehemiah movement seeks to support will take time to emerge, and since the movement is only six years old it is too early to evaluate long-term results. But in terms of reach, they are working with a large church group of 800 pastors and more than 2000 congregations across India, so there is potential for impact on a significant scale, and future evaluations will hopefully be able to measure more tangible outcomes.

Assess the national context before tackling corruption head-on

In countries with little democratic space, or where Christians are persecuted, tackling corruption head-on may just result in further persecution, with little or no reduction in corruption. Lack of democracy and persecution of Christians often go hand in hand, though there are some striking exceptions such as Swaziland (were democracy is quite restricted, but Christians are not specifically persecuted) and India (which is much more democratic, but where Christians are increasingly persecuted for their faith). In those contexts, the best practical contribution for Christians may be to quietly support small-scale activities that improve literacy and build a sense of community. In time, this may help grassroots organisations to form, and those organisations, when the state becomes less oppressive, can start to advocate against corruption.

However, there are many countries, largely in the Americas, Australasia, the Caribbean, Europe, and parts of sub-Saharan Africa, where Christians have enough freedom to confront corruption head on. Historical and contemporary examples from different parts of the world show that Christians can help to control corruption through both bottom-up and top-down initiatives.

Advocate for less corruption in government (a bottom-up approach)

A useful starting point here is Gordon & Lawson's booklet 'Why Advocate on Governance and Corruption' (available free online – please see 'recommended further reading' at the end of this book.)

Case study: The Association for a More Just Society (Honduras)

The Honduran organisation The Association for a More Just Society (AJS) was founded in 1998 by a group of four Hondurans and a North American couple working in Honduras. AJS describe themselves as 'Christians dedicated to making Honduras' system of laws and government work properly to do justice for the poor, and inspiring other Christians to do justice'. Their anti-corruption work encompasses land rights, investigative journalism, reform of education and public health services, a corruption hotline and legal assistance. Their efforts in education reform have produced impressive results:

> Before 2010, children in Honduras met for school an average of only 125 days per year – far fewer than the 200 days required by law. Teachers showed up to teach sporadically, or not at all, without consequence. Though Honduras was spending more per capita on education than any other Latin American country, test results were the lowest in Latin America. Corruption and poor management in the education system was hurting Honduras' future – its children.

> In 2009, AJS helped form a coalition that mobilised thousands of volunteers, mostly parents, to record students' days in class and the attendance of their teachers. They used this information, along with detailed reports created by AJS investigators, to pressure the government for change.

> These efforts prompted decisive change from the Honduran government, including the firing of the Minister of Education. As a result of these reforms, days in class jumped from 120 on average to over 200 and teachers' absence from classrooms dropped from 26% to 1%. These changes make a difference. Honduras's third grade math test scores jumped five places in less than five years, now 10th out of 15 in Latin America. Children are learning more and learning better.

These claims are supported by a UNESCO study of 15 Latin American countries, which found that Honduras had jumped from 15th to 10th place for third grade scores over the period 2000 to 2013. The improvements for third graders were greater than those seen for older students, which suggests that the reforms promoted by AJS, which were targeted mainly at younger students, played an important part in the observed improvements.

Reform government and business through Christian leaders who work within them (a top-down approach)

Unfortunately, there is no guarantee that Christians who hold positions of power will use their role to fight corruption. But if they are well prepared, carefully taught, and operate within a context of spiritual accountability, they can make a big difference.

Case study: The Fellowship of Christians in Government (the Philippines)

Since 2005 the Fellowship of Christians in Government (FOCIG) has been pursuing a top-down strategy in the Philippines. Recognising the huge influence of the military, they began there, by asking the Secretary of National Defence to approve a proposal to conduct moral values training for the generals who lead the Armed Forces of the Philippines. About half the generals agreed to attend, and half of them made a personal commitment to Christ.

Generals who have converted to Jesus have started to refuse large kickbacks on contracts for military hardware, and taken a zero-tolerance approach to extra-judicial killings. Probably the most dramatic impact of this approach came during the Philippines Presidential election in 2010. The army

> Generals who have converted to Jesus have started to refuse large kickbacks on contracts for military hardware, and taken a zero-tolerance approach to extra-judicial killings.

chief at that time, General Bangit, had a nominal Catholic background, but committed himself to Jesus in 2005 after attending the FOCIG moral values training seminars.

In 2010 he was offered the opportunity to lead a military junta, on the condition that he would lead a military coup in the event of victory by the reforming candidate Benigno Aquino. However, General Bangit maintained that his duty as a Christian was to protect the Philippine Constitution, so he refused the offer to lead a military junta and instead helped to ensure there was a free and fair election by ordering the army to assist in the distribution of electronic voting machines.

Benigno Aquino was duly elected and, during his time as president, Transparency International's ranking of the Philippines among countries in the Asia Pacific region rose from 25th out of 33 in 2010, to 11th out of 27 countries in 2014, before falling back to 18th out of 30 countries by the end of his term in 2016. Such dramatic changes in any country's CPI ranking are rarely seen over such a short period of time.

One of the limitations of this approach to reform is the relatively high rate of turnover among the Philippine generals, who typically spend only a few years in post before their compulsory retirement at age 56. Another challenge is the constant threat of resurgent political forces opposed to good governance. The Philippine constitution limits presidents to serving a single six-year term and in 2016 Benigno Aquino was succeeded by Rodrigo Duterte. He does not share Aquino's reputation for integrity, and this is reflected in Transparency International's ranking the Philippines, which has continued to slide backwards. However, these challenges are not a reason to give up, but merely illustrations of the reality that sustained improvements in political order usually take decades, not years, to achieve.

A world without corruption

REVELATION 21:23-7 paints a wonderful picture of the destiny of the world as it describes rulers and nations living in right relationship with God and acting with integrity:

The glory of God gives the city light, and the Lamb is its lamp. The nations will walk by its light, and the kings of the earth will bring their splendour into it ... The glory and honour of the nations will be brought into it. Nothing impure will enter it, nor will anyone who does what is shameful or deceitful, but only those whose names are written in the Lamb's book of life.

While we wait for God's decisive victory over corruption, he expects us to use whatever power we have in the here and now to demonstrate his generous justice. And whatever challenges or opposition we face in the fight against corruption, the final outcome is assured.

The Faith and Public Integrity Network

If reading this booklet has inspired you to get involved in helping to fight corruption please visit the website of the Faith and Public Integrity Network and introduce yourself.

https://fpinetwork.wordpress.com/

FPIN was established in 2016 as a learning community of Christian organisations striving to counter corruption in their local communities. It publishes country profiles, case profiles, and other anti-corruption resources, and welcomes new members who are seeking to develop a Christian faith-based approach to this important task.

Recommended further reading

Allaby, Martin

2013: *Inequality, Corruption and the Church: Challenges and opportunities in the global church* Oxford: Regnum

Berkley Center For Religion, Peace & World Affairs

2009: *Faith and Good Governance: Towards Strengthening Global Coalitions* Washington DC: Georgetown University

Gordon, Graham and Lawson, Melissa

2012: *Why Advocate on Governance and Corruption?* Teddington: Tearfund

https://learn.tearfund.org/~/media/files/tilz/topics/why_advocate_on_governance_and_corruption.pdf

Laver, Roberto

2010: *"Good news" in the fight against corruption* Review of Faith and International Affairs 8/4:49-57

Sebahene, Alfred

2017: *Corruption mocking at justice: A theological and ethical perspective on public life in Tanzania and its implications for the Anglican Church of Tanzania* Carlisle: Langham Monographs

Stückelberger, Christoph

2010: *Corruption-Free Churches are Possible: Experiences, Values, Solutions* Geneva: Globethics.net *https://www.globethics.net/documents/4289936/13403252/Focus-Series_02_Corruption_Christoph_text.pdf*

Tearfund UK

Various learning resources on governance and corruption, available at https://learn.tearfund.org/resources/policy_and_research/governance_and_corruption/

MICAH Global is a world-wide movement of Christian organisations, institutions and individuals networking and acting together towards a transforming and integral mission that sees the church as an agent of change in every community.

We are a catalyst, a movement and a network for transforming mission with a special focus on mobilising a united response towards reducing poverty, addressing injustice and enabling reconciliation and conflict resolution around the world.

We work to deepen the understanding and application of integral mission as expressed through ministry responses such as relief, rehabilitation, development, creation care, justice, and peace-making and reconciliation initiatives.

Established in 2001, Micah now has over 800 members in 93 countries. Our vision inspires us towards the realisation of communities living life in all its fullness, free from extreme poverty, injustice or conflict.

> Micah Global's motivating call to action is expressed in Micah 6:8. "What does the Lord require of you? To act justly and to love mercy, and to walk humbly with your God."

Connect with us www.micahglobal.org